MONTESSORI MARCY

"WITHOUT A SOUND"

MARGARET A. KLING A.M.I

Autobiography

"Montessori Marcy"
Without a Sound

First, and most important, I am a parent like all of you! I am also an educator, Montessori director, and now a writer. I come from a long line of teachers in my family. I chose Montessori education as a specialty. My mother, Rosemary Simpson, was an elementary teacher for 20 years and was never quite satisfied with the confines of always teaching from a given curriculum. She researched Montessori education in the early 1970s and founded the first Montessori school in Delaware. The business was successful, and many of our parents and students today remember my mother and her undying dedication to the education of young children.

My mother always thought I would make a good teacher. The timing was right for my mother to consider retiring after 25 years of teaching and owning the Dover Montessori School. I stepped up, completed my Master's in Montessori Ed, and bought the family business. I was never happier! I grew the business and enrolled approximately 50 students each school year. We also had a very successful summer camp.

Thousands of children have attended our school, and I am very proud of our reputation in the Community. When I bought the business and became the director, I changed the name to Dover Montessori Country Day Academy or DMCDA.

I have been teaching, owning, and operating this small business for 30 years. However, no one saw the pandemic coming, and I was forced to close early in March of 2019.

I had to make one of the biggest but perhaps the best decision to sell my business. This was an end of an era in my life but the beginning of a new chapter.

I have always wanted to write children's books. I thought, *what a great idea!* Parents at home with their children most of the time, due to the pandemic, would enjoy implementing some "Montessori Marcy" techniques at home. This book is a series designed for parents to extract helpful tips while managing their children every day at home.

This book, "Without a Sound," has many exercises children can do successfully without much assistance from parents, using household items to create interesting games, such as balancing items on a tray while walking on a line.

I hope that parents enjoy implementing these activities with their children, and they start to put down the screens and electronic devices. Realizing the benefit of daily living exercises, we reference practical life Montessori lessons.

"Montessori Marcy" is always ready to learn something new! Join us for our next adventure!

Author,

Margaret A. Kling A.M.I.

"Montessori Marcy"
Without a Sound

Author and Montessori Professional;
Margaret A. Kling A.M.I.

Thoughts for Parents

1. Telling a story can be fun and interactive.

2. Talk to your child about sounds; where do they come from?

3. This book can be utilized to present how to control movement.

4. Each activity will engage your child in a thought process: how to achieve the desired result, perfect a new skill, and ultimately exercise self-control.

5. Your child will want to repeat these exercises, come up with their own ideas, and various ways to implement each activity.

A Child Reacts to Everyday Activities Without Sound

There are many things we do in our daily routine that make a variety of sounds.

Children are moving so fast; at times, it is difficult to slow them down. Young children will find this fascinating and challenging to do multiple tasks required with their body in motion and all while not making a sound. The idea behind the book is to teach self-control at an early age. As the book progresses, there are more difficult and interesting tasks.

How Do We Distinguish Sounds?

If you close your eyes, sounds become more emphasized and more distinguishable. As adults, we have the capability of hearing many sounds and can verify the origin of each sound. We can distinguish soft or loud, for example. All sounds can be detected and categorized. Ask a child:

- What kind of sounds do you hear?
- Do you think these sounds are inside or outside?
- What kind of sounds do you hear when people are walking?
- Can you walk across the floor and not make a sound?
- What kind of sounds do you hear that are outside? Are they loud or soft sounds?
- Tell me, what can make a loud sound?
- What kind of loud sound can you make?

How to Introduce the Concept: Opening and closing a door.

Activities Without a Sound: Whispering your name.

Walking across a room.

Placing an item on a table.

Balancing an item on a tray.

Walking on a line.

Children like to play games; children are naturally curious about body movements. Children have a natural desire to experience control. If they walk slowly and carefully, no one will be able to hear their footsteps; this is a wonderful way for young children to slow down and concentrate on their next move.

A preliminary activity presents an opportunity for examination of a particular movement by a child. An immediate intrigue develops as the task is repeated for satisfaction and perfection.

The child then becomes focused on the idea of controlling movement in accordance with the required task, such as balancing an item on a tray or walking on a line.

It is fun to observe children. Our observation throughout this book will help gain some insight as to how children are naturally intrigued and motivated to control their movements. In fact, parents will be excited to know that these strategies work.

Children enjoy these exercises and will develop a desire to repeat the exercises on their own without any assistance or prompting.

Balancing, as we know, requires perseverance and the ability to maintain focus. Children naturally want to test their skills over and over, knowing the outcome could be unfavorable. As adults, we can regulate the selection of preliminary activities to include variations for an additional challenge. For example, let children balance a non-breakable item on the center of the tray and walk across the room. Also, parents can introduce an item that requires care, put it on the center of the tray, and let the child walk around a mat or a table. The child will naturally slow down the progression of the exercise to achieve the desired result; the balance will occur, and ultimately self-control. This feeling of being able to enhance our ability is at the core of our delight. Just like sports are popular and fun to play, we are also learning to acquire a new skill.

I hope that every parent reading this book with their child will gain some new insights and enjoy implementing these techniques while spending quality time at home. Every parent can use "tips" on how to make everyday routine into teachable moments that are fun and do not require any screens or electronic devices.

"Montessori Marcy"
Without a Sound

As I woke up, I could hear the birds singing, lawnmowers making that sound they make, and Mr. Filmore's dog barking.

Mr. Filmore is our neighbor, who likes to walk his dog early in the morning. I closed my eyes and just listened; I could hear many sounds. Most of the sounds were ones I had heard before. I kept my eyes closed and waited for something different that I had never heard before. Ms. Clarisse, my teacher, asked us to practice listening for inside and outside sounds. I like to play games, and it is fun to be quiet as a mouse sometimes. Suddenly, I heard, "Marcy, time for breakfast."

Now that is a familiar sound. I was waiting for a different sound.

Slam! What was that? My older sister, Charlotte, slamming her bedroom door. That was a really loud sound. As I got dressed, I wondered what it would be like if I could close my bedroom door without a sound? My mom said that Charlotte slams her door on purpose. I did it! I figured out how to turn the knob ever so slightly, and closed the door without making any noise! Hey, it worked! Now I have something to tell my friends

and Ms. Clarisse today. I could not wait to go to school! Ms. Clarisse calls me 'Montessori Marcy.' She says I am always ready for a new lesson. I am five years old, so I can give lessons to the younger students too! I like to be the 'teacher helper.' Today, I will show Ms. Clarisse my new way to close a door without making a sound.

I am a pre-school student at Lakeview Montessori Academy. As I walked up to the front door of the school, I thought of all the doors I could practice on that day and show my friends.

"Good Morning, Marcy," said Ms. Clarisse. "How are you today?"

"I am great!" I said in a loud voice. Then, I used my whisper voice and said, "I have something to tell you, Ms. Clarisse."

"Oh, I cannot wait to hear all about it," Ms. Clarisse whispered back. "Would you like to sit next to me during line time today?"

"Yes, thank you," I said.

"Let's get started. Hello, my name is Ms. Clarisse, and what is yours?"

This was a game we played at line time. Everyone got to say their name, and we tried to remember the person before us. This time Ms. Clarisse said her name very softly, almost no one could hear; I had to really listen, and it was fun. We went all the way around the room, and everyone said their name very softly. Ms. Clarisse said, "Now we will say our names in a normal

tone." It was different. Next, we all took turns saying our names in a loud voice. That was the most fun. Everyone laughed!

"I think Marcy has something she would like to share with us today," said Ms. Clarisse.

I was so excited to tell everyone. "Remember, Ms. Clarisse told us to go home and practice listening for different sounds?

"Well, I closed my eyes for a long time. Then I heard it...a very loud 'slam.' My sister Charlotte is eleven and goes around the house slamming all the doors shut. My mom says she does it on purpose, but your dad and I have chosen to just ignore it. Maybe she will stop.

"I can close the door without making a sound! I turn the knob ever so slightly and push the door closed, so there is no sound at all. Everyone can take turns and try it!"

"Marcy, you can choose someone who is sitting their best way to come up and try to close the door without a sound. Next, you may walk across the room without a sound and find your work." This was not easy; to walk all the way across the room and not make a sound. I really thought about how to move slowly and tiptoe very quietly. I pretended there was a sleeping bear in the middle of the floor, if I was not careful, well, so far, the bear did not wake up! Everyone tried closing the door and tip toeing across the room just like me, watching my every move! It was the best day ever!

As soon as I got home, I told my mom and dad what had happened at school. They smiled and said, "Maybe I could teach my new game to Charlotte."

When Mom asked me to help set the table for dinner, I had another game to play. At school, I learned the correct way to carry a chair. Ms. Clarisse showed us how to clasp the seat of the chair with thumbs on top and four fingers underneath. I can now carry any chair and put it under the table without a sound. I like to play this game at home when setting the table for dinner. I make sure to place all the chairs without a sound. Also I would place each plate on the table without a sound.

Next, I would place each knife, fork, and spoon the same, without a sound. Mom said I am big enough to carry a glass of water to each place at the table too. I must walk slowly and make sure our dog, Sophie, was not going to run around or jump next to me. I decided Sophie could stay in my room until dinner was over, then I would take her for a nice walk outside. "You are such a helper, Marcy," my mom said. "I did not even know you were there; it was so quiet." Mom and Dad say peace and quiet are all they want sometimes. Not sure why they say this, I think it is just something grown-ups say. Clara's parents say the same thing; maybe because Clara's parents have five kids in the house. Now that I think of it, every time I visit Clara, a lot is going on all the time and much more noise. At our house, it is only my mom and dad, Charlotte, and me. Oh, and my dog, Sophie, of course.

Now it is time to take my dog, Sophie, for a walk outside. It is my favorite time of the year, Mom says, "Please, wear a coat outside." I like the smell in the air and the sound the leaves make under my feet as we walk along the sidewalk. The leaves are many colors. I like to collect leaves; the red ones are my favorite. I thought I would trace them when I got home or do a leaf rubbing, like the ones I do at school. "Come on, Sophie, time to go home now."

Sophie and I walk every day. I put a little doggie sweater on her so she can stay warm like me.

Outside, sounds are different, usually louder. For example, cars and buses going by or Mr. Filmore's leaf blower and lawnmower. Ms. Clarisse said, "We live in such a noisy world filled with sounds of television and electronics that we do not have time to enjoy the silence."

I think she is right. My favorite time of the day is when I am upstairs in my room, lying on my bed with my dog Sophie just being as still as I can be, not moving. I can see my chest rise as I take each breathe and feel Sophie's tummy go in and out. She is breathing too, but quiet, like me.

The next day will be a big day. Ms. Clarisse has new lessons to show everyone. She explains all about how to balance an object on a tray while walking. Ms. Clarisse usually starts with the students who are five years old in the class. I am excited because I know she will pick me!

"Good morning, class," said Ms. Clarisse. "I have something to show you. We have already practiced carrying our work on a tray to a table. Now we are going to see if we can walk to a table while balancing this plastic cup with water in the middle of the tray; we will also try to place the tray carefully on the table without a sound. We will start with Johnathan, then Marcy, Audrey, and Sebastian." I looked around the room, and everyone watched as Johnathan picked up the tray with the cup of water in the middle and started walking across the room. His eyes were fixed on the cup of water. I noticed how he started to walk faster. Ms. Clarisse said to everyone: "Remember, this is not a race."

Johnathan got to the other side of the room and put the tray down without spilling any water. Everyone clapped. "Marcy, would you like to come and hold the tray?" I got up slowly and walked to pick up the tray with a cup of water in the middle. I remembered how to hold the tray: thumbs locked on top, four fingers securely underneath, and the tray just touching the middle of my chest. I looked straight ahead, not at the cup of water. I knew if I walked slowly to the table, held my tray in place, the cup would not go over. I was right! It worked perfectly! Everyone clapped. I wanted to do it again, but it was Audrey's turn. Ms. Clarisse invited Audrey to come up. Audrey picked up the tray and looked down at her feet as she started to walk, but the tray went sideways, and the cup of water went on the floor. Ms. Clarisse said, "Let's clean this up for the next person."

Audrey looked a little sad. Ms. Clarisse said, "We all have to practice; Audrey will get another turn." Audrey smiled.

Sebastian was eager to try to balance the tray and walk across the room. He jumped up, walked over quickly, and grabbed the tray. The cup of water rocked back and forth but did not go over. Sebastian held the tray carefully and looked straight ahead. He walked quickly to the table and put the tray down, saying, "I won!"

"Remember, this is not a race. What have we learned?" asked Ms. Clarisse. We each got to say what we learned about doing the exercise. I said that balancing a cup of water on a tray and walking was not as easy as it looked. Audrey said she would like to have another turn to practice. Jonathan said he probably looked at the cup of water and not where he was going. Sebastian kept saying how he could get to the table faster than anyone. It was fun.

I was looking forward to our next exercise and the last one for the day. We would all take a turn, walking on the line and carrying an item on a tray. Our line was one big circle around the classroom. We could choose any small item in the room to place on the tray. Ms. Clarisse said, "If you walk slowly on the line and balance the tray, the item will not move out of place." I could see that this would take some practice. We all got to select a small item and began walking on the line with our tray. Ms. Clarisse spaced us out on the line so we would not bump into anyone.

I love to learn, new Montessori lessons are always fun. After the classroom activities, I have even more fun and practice at home too! There are lots of items I can find to put on my tray; I could practice walking around chairs and tables. Lots to do, all without a sound! I am 'Montessori Marcy!' I can do anything! I just need to remember to keep practicing and never give up!

So, join me, Montessori Marcy, for my next adventure! There is so much to learn and explore every day!

Made in the USA
Monee, IL
12 March 2022

92828330R00017